About the Book

As a small girl, Amelia Earhart loved to do exciting things—whether it was racing down a steep hill on a sled, traveling around the country by train with her family because her father was a lawyer for the railroad, or seeing her first airplane from her father's shoulders at a country fair. Amelia was a "tomboy." She was the curious one, the girl whose yearbook picture carried the caption "Girl in Brown Who Walks Alone."

Amelia Earhart was to grow up to become the first woman to cross the Atlantic Ocean by plane, the first woman to fly the Atlantic alone, and the first person to solo between Hawaii and California.

Peggy Mann presents the exciting story of this courageous young woman and the record-breaking flights that she undertook are all here in vivid detail.

Also by Peggy Mann
CLARA BARTON
Battlefield Nurse
THE STREET OF THE FLOWER BOXES
WHEN CARLOS CLOSED THE STREET
THE CLUBHOUSE
THAT NEW BABY
THE BOY WITH A BILLION PETS
THE TWENTY-FIVE-CENT FRIEND

Amelia Earhart
FIRST LADY OF FLIGHT

by Peggy Mann

illustrated by Kiyo Komoda

Coward, McCann & Geoghegan, Inc.
New York

For another great woman,
my mother, Edna Mann.

© 1970 by Peggy Mann

All rights reserved. This book, or parts thereof, may not be reproduced in any form without permission in writing from the publishers. Published simultaneously in the Dominion of Canada by Longmans Canada, Limited, Toronto.

Library of Congress Catalog Card Number: 71-106932

Printed in the United States of America

Third Impression
SBN: GB 698-30008-4

Amelia Earhart

1

It was like flying! The big hill was a slick sheet of ice. She was lying flat on her new sled. The wind stung her face. Her hair whipped out behind her.

Then she saw him. The junkman, driving his horse and cart, was coming out from a side road. Her sled was hurtling straight toward him. The junkman, she knew, was deaf. His horse was wearing blinders. There was no way to warn them. She tried to turn the sled. But the hill was too icy. If she rolled off, the riderless sled might crash into the horse's legs. She shoved, with all her strength, at the steering bar. And she held her breath. She might just make it!

Like a shooting star, the sled hurtled underneath the horse's belly, between his fore legs and his hind legs.

At the bottom of the hill she looked up. The horse and wagon were plodding on along the road. Did the junkman even know what had happened? Probably not.

She began to laugh with relief, excitement, exhilaration. Then she got off her sled and started the long climb up the icy hill.

It was the sled which had saved her: the wonderful steel-runnered boy's sled which Papa had given her for Christmas.

Grandma Otis had not approved, of course. (Grandma Otis, it seemed, did not approve of *any*thing Papa did.) "Why, Edwin!" she'd exclaimed when Amelia tore off the wrapping paper and the sleek wooden sled lay exposed. "Whatever can you be *thinking* of! First giving the child a *football* for Christmas. And now—a *boy's* sled!"

"But I love it!" Amelia had cried. "I can go belly whopping on this kind of sled."

Girls, of course, were supposed to ride on heavy "safe" sleds, with high sides and thick wooden runners. Girls were supposed to ride sitting up in a ladylike position. But girls' sleds were almost impossible to steer. And if she'd been sitting up, she would have crashed right into the horse's belly. Either his ribs would have been broken or her head. *Probably his ribs!* she thought. Grandma Otis was forever calling her a stubborn, hardheaded child.

All activity had stopped on the big hill. The children were watching her, waiting. All but her sister Muriel who came running, sliding toward her.

"We thought you'd be *killed!*" She threw her arms tight around Amelia's neck.

"You'll choke me," Amelia laughed. But she felt suddenly like crying. Muriel didn't often *show* her love like this. Especially not right out—in front of everyone.

"Come on, Pidge," she said. "Let's go. They're all—looking."

"You *can't* get killed!" Muriel declared stoutly. "Because who would I have left?"

"Don't worry," Amelia said. "Nothing's going to kill me. Not ever. Come on. Help me pull this sled."

"Were you scared?" Muriel wanted to know as they started up the hill together.

"Scared?" said Amelia. "No. It was—exciting. Besides," she added, "when you go *fast* like that, you don't have time to be scared."

2

They had always been close, Amelia Earhart and her sister, Muriel. They *had* to be close.

Papa was a lawyer who worked for the railroad, settling claims. This meant he traveled a lot. When they were little, the girls had gone with their parents. But when Amelia was six years old and Muriel three, the sisters had been sent to live with their grandparents in the big white house on a hill overlooking the Missouri River. It was time for Amelia to start school. She *had* to settle in one place. So Atchison, Kansas, had become hometown.

Mama came from time to time to visit her girls and her parents.

Papa's visits were fewer and seemed endlessly far between. But at least when he was with <u>them</u>, he was really *with* them! He took his girls adventuring, exploring the sandstone caves on the bluffs of the Missouri River. He played football with them, baseball, basketball. Even taught them how to hurdle over the back fence.

"You're ruining those children!" Grandma Otis often told him. "Turning them into regular tomboys! Look at them! Running about in bloomers and blouses when every other girl in town wears a proper dress. Too bad you didn't have sons instead of daughters, Edwin!"

But Amelia knew that her father loved them just as they were. He never wished that they *were* boys. It was just that he didn't want them to miss out on a lot of the

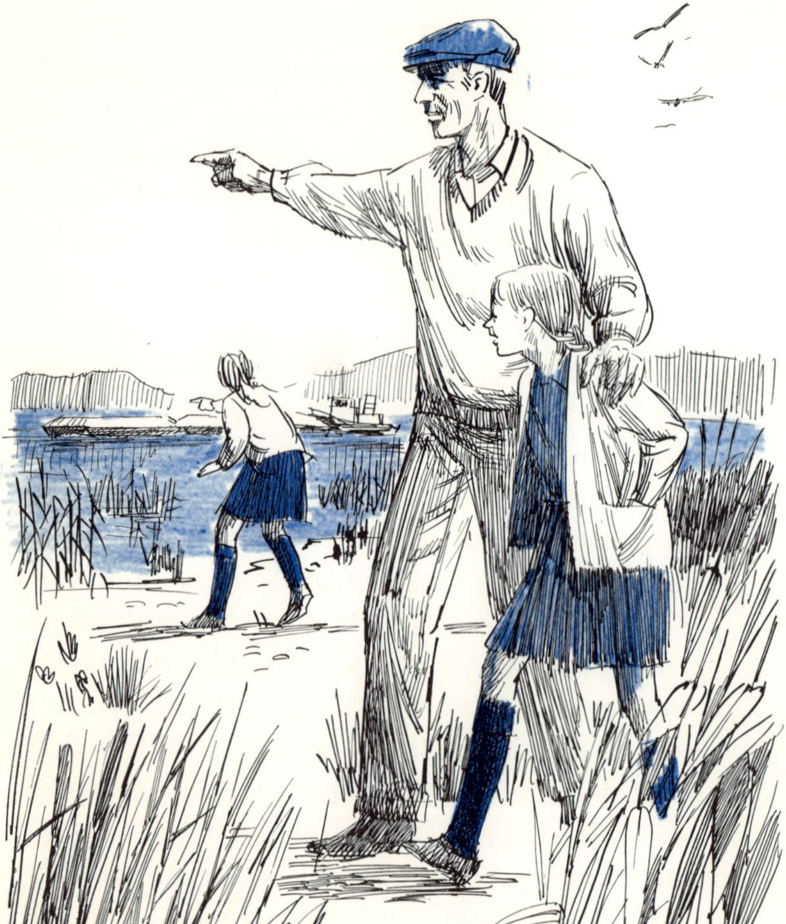

fun that boys had—fun which was forbidden for "ladylike" girls.

And Mama agreed with Papa about this. It was she who had sent them the bloomers and middy blouses. "These are for you to wear for play," she had written. "I'm tired of so many ruined dresses." But after the strict sentences she'd added, "Have a lot of fun in them. Love, Mama."

Amelia and Muriel were happy enough with their grandparents. And when Grandma Otis tried *too* hard to turn the girls into "little ladies," Grandpa, with something of a twinkle in his eyes, would remind his wife that, in fact, *she* had not always been so "ladylike" herself. Indeed, if she *had* been, Grandpa claimed, he'd never have married her in the first place!

"I wanted a real pioneer bride," Grandpa Otis said. "And I got myself one."

He often told the girls stories about those early days: their trip in a covered wagon from Philadelphia to Kansas right after the Civil War.

"I wish *I* had lived then," Amelia once said wistfully to her grandfather. She pictured herself galloping across the plains bareback on a horse, while a tribe of whooping, war-painted Indians thundered on the trail behind her. There was excitement in those days. But today everything was so safe and—civilized.

"I was born at the wrong time," she announced. "Nobody can be a real pioneer anymore!"

3

It was the most special day of her whole life.

July 24, 1907. Her ninth birthday.

She and Pidge were staying with Mama and Papa for the summer vacation. And Papa had promised—as a birthday treat—that he would take his daughters to the Iowa State Fair. The girls had never been to a big fair before. This one was everything they had expected—and much more. Like a small county fair blown up a thousand times in colors, sounds, crowds and—excitement.

Where to go first? What to do? Barkers stood at sideshow booths shouting out, "Ladeeeez and gents..." "Right this way..." "Step right up . . ." "See the remarkable ... "Witness the unforgettable..." "Three tries for a penny . . ." "Don't miss the sensational...."

At one booth they shot pellets at moving cardboard Indians. And Amelia won a prize: a tin candlestick. At another booth they tossed rope rings onto a pole. And Amelia won a stuffed blue dog.

"They must know it's your birthday, Melia!" Papa laughed. "Letting you win all those presents."

"What do you mean, *letting* me!" Amelia demanded. "I've got good aim, is all!"

The bright, jangling rhythms of music started up suddenly. "Oh, Papa!" Pidge cried. "Let's go on the merry-go-round! Hurry!" So they ran down the causeway, their balloons trailing behind them.

The carousel was huge, painted in bright

colors, and already crowded with children astride the charging wooden horses. Amelia climbed on a coal-black stallion, put her feet in the stirrups, and took hold of the reins. She was barely in the saddle when the carousel started to move—slowly at first, then fast, faster. The black stallion plunged up and down. She reached for the gold ring, straining out of her saddle. She almost fell off, but she had touched the ring! Perhaps next time—

Suddenly a loudspeaker voice rode in over the music. "Ladeeez and gentlemen, in one half hour the most spectacular event of the fair! The flying airplane will take off into the sky! Don't miss it! At the airfield near the south end of the fairground."

The flying airplane? What on earth was *that*?

When the music stopped and the mounts came to a standstill, Amelia and Pidge ran to their father. "Papa," Amelia cried, "buy more tickets! I'm *sure* I'll get the gold ring next time!"

But it seemed that Mr. Earhart had something *he* wanted to see. "Did you hear the announcement about the flying airplane? *That's* something we don't want to miss!" He took a girl firmly by each hand and started off down the causeway. It wasn't easy, but he managed to get them to the South Field without stopping at a single booth.

A crowd had already gathered, encircling the high wire fence.

"Papa, we can't see a *thing!*" Amelia objected.

Her father pointed to the sky. "Can you see up there?"

She nodded.

"Well, all you need to do is keep watching the sky."

"What *is* an airplane, Papa?" said Amelia.

"A contraption which flies in the air. It has a gasoline engine. And a man drives it. Kind of like a flying automobile."

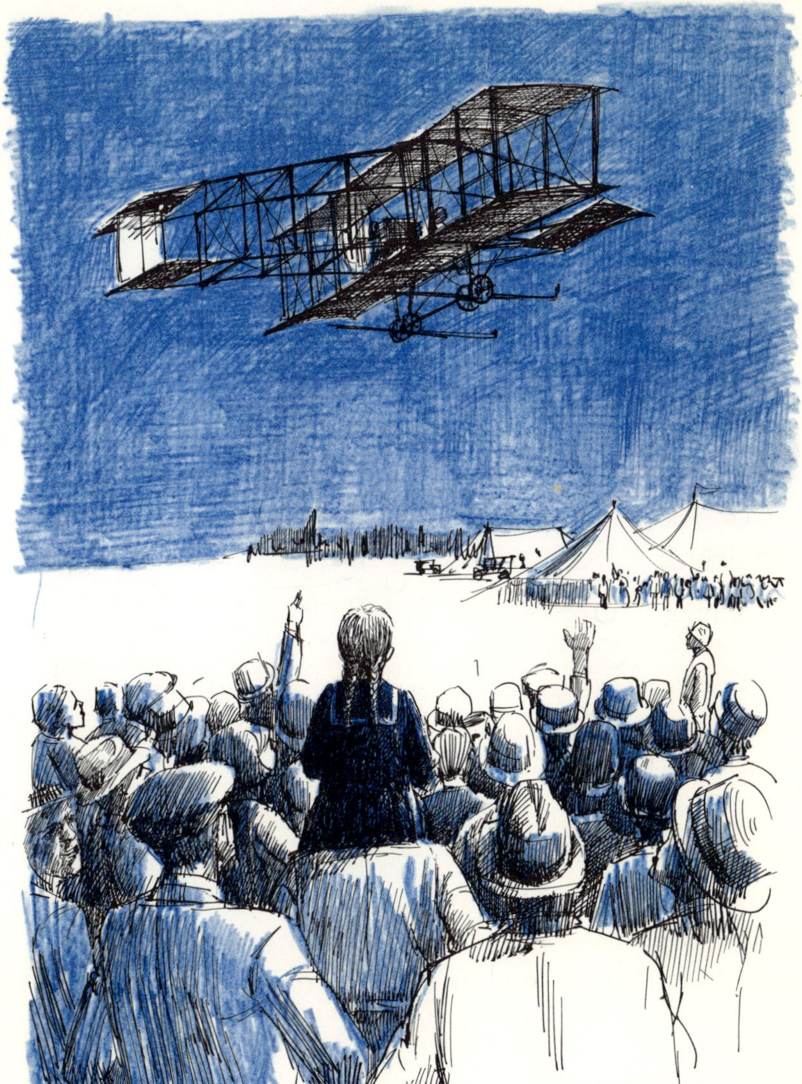

"Papa!" Amelia demanded. "Lift me on your shoulders. I want to see the airplane right now!"

"That's easier said than done, miss!" said Mr. Earhart. Nevertheless he hoisted his tall, nine-year-old daughter onto his back.

Amelia gasped. "You don't mean he's going up into the sky in *that!*" she exclaimed. "He'll get killed."

The flying airplane was made of wood, held together with rusty wire. There were two broad thin boards, one above the other, attached by skinny pieces of wood. A man, wearing goggles, sat between these two winglike boards, his feet on a cross bar which reminded Amelia of the steering bar on her Flexible Flyer sled. A bulky motor was set on a seat behind the man. The tail of the airplane looked like Baily Waggoner's box kite. And the whole thing rested on three wheels, two in front, one in back.

"Papa!" Amelia cried. "It's beginning!"

There were great spluttering cracking

sounds as a man turned a flat wooden board attached to the motor. Then the board began to whirl—by itself. And after a moment the flying airplane started moving slowly down the field, pushed by two men in overalls.

The noises from the motor were now like rapid gunshots. The thing was moving more quickly along the stubble and grass. Then it was speeding. "Papa!" Amelia screamed out. "It's going up into the *air!*" But her words were lost in the sudden cheering which arose from the crowd.

Amelia slid down from her father's shoulders. She could see perfectly well now from the ground, for the peculiar contraption of wood, wire, and wheels was in the *sky*. It was charging along right above them. She stared up in stunned silence, her eyes and her mouth wide open, as the airplane circled the field like a giant, clumsy, noisy bird.

"I *told* you it was something wonderful!"

said Mr. Earhart proudly, as though he himself had engineered the whole event.

"You were right, Papa!" Amelia exclaimed. "It's the most exciting thing I've ever watched in my whole entire life!"

4

Amelia couldn't stop thinking about the flying airplane.

Back in Atchison one of her favorite games had been maptraveling. The two sisters and their cousins, Kathy and Lucy, would sit in the old carriage in the corner of Grandpa's barn. Amelia would open her geography book, close her eyes and put her finger onto the page. Then the foursome would travel to the spot she had selected.

Her favorite map was Africa; she loved

the mysterious-sounding names: Khartoum, Timbuktu, Ngami, El Fasher, Zanzibar. On their last trip the old carriage had been a boat. They were exploring the Lualaba River, on their way to search for diamond mines in the Mountains of the Moon, when suddenly they'd been attacked by Ba-Nagala cannibals. They'd escaped the boiling caldron in the nick of time on the back of an elephant— whom they had, fortunately, tamed on another expedition.

The old carriage, which they could rock or sway, became a ship, a stagecoach, a river raft—as the situation and the girls' imagination required.

But now, suddenly, all of Amelia's imaginary traveling took place in an airplane.

She wondered, of course, how the plane worked: what kept it up in the air. Papa would be able to explain. He was away now on another trip. But when he came home, he would sit down with her and make all the mysteries quite clear. Papa, Amelia was convinced, knew about *every*thing. He had probably read every book ever written.

Papa finally returned home. But it seemed even *he* did not know too much about airplanes. He'd read, of course, about the Wright brothers, Orville and Wilbur, who had invented the airplane four years ago.

"Orville was thirty-six at the time," Mr. Earhart told Amelia. "Wilbur was thirty-two. The Flying Fools people used to call them. Camping out on Kill Devil Hill in the middle of winter. Trying to fly some crazy machine into the air. If God had meant men to fly, the townspeople said, He would have given them wings."

"Maybe He meant to," Amelia commented. "He just didn't get around to it. So the Wright brothers did it for Him."

Mr. Earhart told his daughter about the Wrights' first successful flight. From the beach at Kitty Hawk, North Carolina. On a cold and windy December morning, Orville was the first to go up in the motor-powered plane. It rose into the air for twelve seconds. And it flew 120 feet—the first airplane ever to fly under its own power!

"No one's laughing at the Wright brothers now," Mr. Earhart concluded. "The government has bought their patents and Orville and Wilbur have an airplane factory in Dayton, Ohio. They make two planes a month. They've also opened a flying school. After all, no use having airplanes if no one knows how to fly them."

"Oh, Papa!" Amelia burst out, "Can *I* go to that school when I grow up?"

Mr. Earhart looked down at his daughter and ruffled her hair fondly. "*That,* Melia," he told her, "is one thing girls can never do! Fly an airplane!"

Amelia stared at her father, hurt and surprised. It was the first time in her life Papa had told her there was something she could not do—because she was a girl! Why *couldn't* a woman drive a plane as well as any man?

But she said nothing more about it. Instead, she went off that afternoon to the public library. If Papa didn't know *how* airplanes flew, then she'd find out for herself!

She loved reading. And she loved science. It, along with geography, were her favorite subjects in school. But despite the fact that she was an excellent reader and got top grades in science, she still found it difficult to understand the magazine articles which the librarian found for her about airplanes. All of them had been written to explain the new subject of aeronautics to adults.

But Amelia did the best she could in puzzling things out. And in bed that night she tried to explain the mysteries to Muriel.

"It works like this, Pidge."

"I am *not* Pidge anymore!" said Muriel. (Her favorite song, which she'd sung over and over at the age of three, was "Little Blue Pigeon." So the family had taken to calling her Pidge. Now, however, at the age of six, Muriel considered herself too big for such baby names.)

"Well, *Muriel,*" said Amelia, "it's like this. Air looks like a bunch of nothing. Right? But really it *is* something. Especially when it's moving. Like wind. Wind will hold a kite up in the sky, right?"

"Right," said Muriel sleepily.

"When there's no wind, the kite falls down. Right?"

"Mmmm," said Muriel.

"Well, the airplane makes its *own* wind. By the spinning propeller. And that wind drags the plane through the air. The faster the propeller goes, the faster the plane goes."

"But you can keep a kite up with*out* any wind!" Muriel announced." If you *run* with it."

"Sure," said Amelia. "Because running makes a kite move. And *that* makes the air move out of the way of the kite. And moving air is thinner than still air. Well, airplane wings are kind of like a kite. And because of the *shape* of the plane wings, the thin air rushes by on top. But the air underneath the plane is thick. Like a *wall* of air. And that helping wall is another thing to hold the plane up in the sky. You see?"

There was no answer from the other bed.

"Pidge," said Amelia. *"Muriel!"* she added, louder.

Her sister was asleep, which was just as well. Because actually Amelia could not have answered any more questions on the matter. How could *invisible* air be thick? Holding up a flimsy paper kite was one thing. But how could air—even thick air—

hold up a full-grown man sitting in a heavy airplane?

To Amelia's mind, however, the mysteries of it all only added to the excitement. Though she still didn't understand very much about why and how a plane flew, there was one thing she did know. She wanted to fly! No matter *what* her father said about girls piloting airplanes, she wanted to try!

Then, lying in the dark, she suddenly

laughed out loud. There was her fate, sounding right out loud in her name! Every term a new teacher called out her name when taking the roll. And every term Amelia had to explain: "My name isn't pronounced that way. It's *spelled* like 'ear.' But it's pronounced 'air.' *Air-heart!*"

"My heart's in the air," she whispered to herself. "That's where!"

And she lay staring out the wide-open window into the night sky—wishing fervently that she would grow up in one fast hurry so that she could learn to fly.

5

It seemed that her childhood wish came true. She did grow up in a hurry.

Before she quite realized how the time had passed, she was twelve years old and graduating from the College Preparatory School in Atchison. It was a steaming hot June day. She and Ginger Parks, wearing white ruffled dresses, long white stockings and high black shoes, were standing on the auditorium stage reciting verses from Macaulay's poem *Horatius*.

Ginger sounded scared to death. Amelia felt frightened too. There were so many people out there in the audience, watching, listening. But they certainly hadn't come to see two frightened schoolgirls whispering words which no one could hear. So Amelia spoke out loudly. And after a while Ginger too took courage.

By the time they came to their favorite verse both girls were sounding loud and clear:

>Then out spake brave Horatius
>>The Captain of the Gate:
>To every man upon this earth
>>Death cometh soon or late.
>And how can man die better
>>Than facing fearful odds
>For the ashes of his fathers,
>>And the temples of his Gods?

They plunged on, through all the seventy stanzas. And walked off the stage to enthusiastic applause.

Then, in a few moments it seemed, the entire graduation program was over. And she, Amelia M. Earhart, was holding her diploma and a beautifully bound copy of Macaulay's *Lays of Ancient Rome.* She had won the book as a prize for Excellence in English Composition—of all things.

She watched the others caught in the excitement of graduation day: Ginger and Tootie and Baily Waggoner. Would she ever see any of her best friends again?

They were all going on to high school in Atchison. But not Amelia, for it had been decided that the Earhart sisters should return to their parents. She would be glad, of course, to be with Mama and Papa again. But she had never realized until right this moment how much she would miss living in Grandpa Otis' big white house on the hill in Atchison, Kansas.

The next four years seemed to speed by as fast as the railway cars the Earhart family were constantly riding. Sometimes they would settle down—in Kansas City . . . Des Moines . . . St. Paul . . . Chicago.

But whenever Papa went on a long trip, he took the girls out of school to go with him. "You'll learn as much by traveling," he told them, "as you will sitting in a classroom. Different things, maybe. But just as valuable."

Amelia and Muriel did not make any close friends, as they had in Atchison. But they made many friends.

It was fun to be able to invite new acquaintances to lunch in one's private railway car, in fact, to make lunch *for* them in the tiny kitchenette. It was like playing house. And Amelia liked trying out new recipes—which she made up herself. Boiled pea pods and cornhusks, for instance. Or manna. She and Muriel spent many long hours on train trips trying to concoct the celestial food which had been dropped from heaven to nourish the children of Israel. Amelia was certain that manna looked like small round muffins; white in color and, of

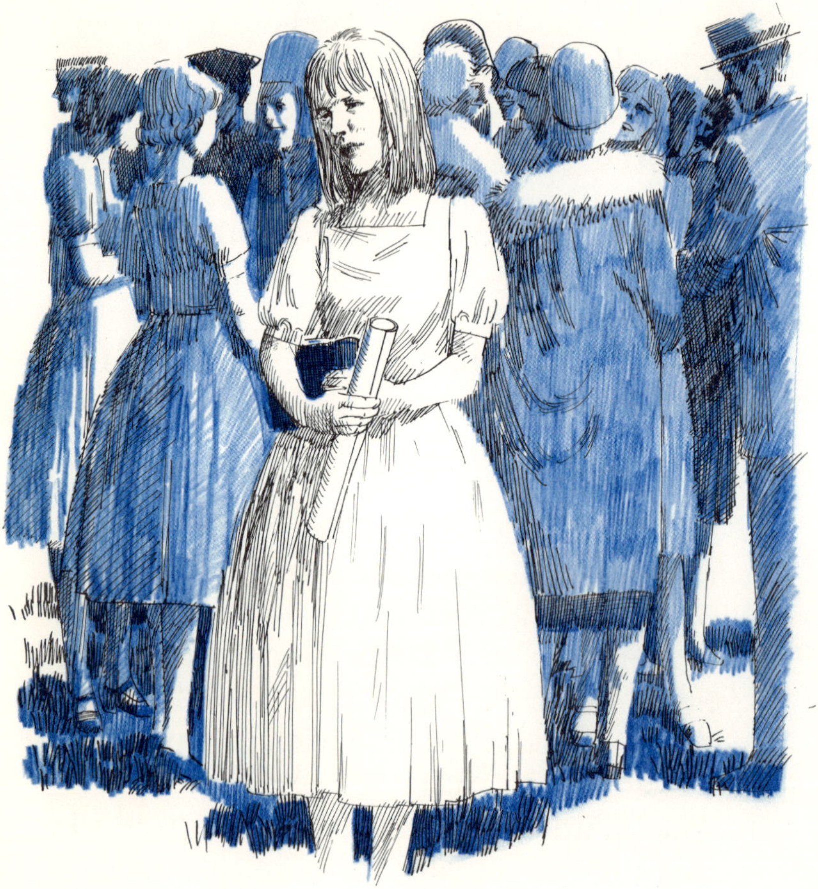

course, resembling angel food cake in taste.

"If we ever could discover the right recipe," she kept insisting, "I'm sure we'd make a fortune. *Everyone* would want to buy manna!"

Within four short years, Amelia went to six high schools in six different cities. She was graduated from Hyde Park High in Chicago.

Again, graduation day held a certain sadness.

"Why don't people like me?" she exclaimed to her mother when they reached home.

"Of course they like you, Melia! Everyone does."

"Look what they wrote about me in the yearbook!" She flipped open the pages, to pictures of boys and girls in the graduating class. Each picture had a complimentary caption beneath it. But underneath hers there was only one sentence: "Girl in Brown Who Walks Alone."

"Is *that* the best they could say about

me!" she demanded. "It makes me sound like some sort of—spook!"

"It's just that they don't know you, darling. After all, you haven't been there very long."

Amelia looked at her mother with wide gray eyes. "Mama, am I very—different from the others?"

Mrs. Earhart laughed a little. "You've always been. A real little tomboy. Yet you've turned into a beautiful girl as well."

"Me? *Beautiful?* Mama! You must need spectacles!"

"Not at all, my love." After a moment, she added, "As far as I can see, it's usually the people who are different who do the most exciting things. But"—she shrugged—"you're old enough now to make of yourself what you will. It's your choice, Amelia. You can be like all the others. Or you can be like you."

"Well—" said Amelia. Then she grinned. "I guess I might as well be me."

6

She leaned into the cold wind, and laughed a little. She was nineteen years old. It was Christmastime. She was in a new city, Toronto. And she was filled with the excitement and joy which traveling—and Christmastime—always brought.

Then her laughter broke off, strangled, in her throat. Four young men—soldiers—were coming down the street on crutches. Each had lost a leg. As they passed her, one of them grinned, but it was the saddest smile

Amelia had ever seen. The other three looked away, as if embarrassed.

She walked on. And on. She forgot about Christmas shopping. The picture of the four young men seemed burned into her brain.

Back home where she was attending Ogontz—a finishing school in Philadelphia—the World War meant handsome young officers who came to the school dances. It meant knitting socks and rolling bandages. Martial music and parades. The war itself was very far away.

But Canada had been at war for four years. Muriel—who was going to college in Toronto—had written in her letters about the soldiers and the suffering. But this was the first living evidence Amelia Earhart had seen.

A few hours later she burst into the hotel room where she and her mother were staying. "I'm not going back to Philadelphia," she announced. "I'm going to work here as a nurse's aide."

"Don't be ridiculous, Melia!" her mother

exclaimed. "You're in your senior year at college. You'll graduate in June. You're not going to stop school now!"

"But *now* is when I'm needed, Mother. I can finish school when the war is over."

Mrs. Earhart knew her daughter, knew that when Amelia really set her mind on something, that was the way it would be.

A few days later Amelia Earhart went up for a Red Cross course as a nurse's aide. And within a few months she was working at Spadina Military Hospital in Toronto.

It was a huge and gloomy place, overcrowded, understaffed. There were beds to be made, rooms to be swept, trays to be carried and collected. Amelia could drive, so they sent her to pick up supplies from the depot. Amelia knew some chemistry, so they allowed her to mix pails of medicine when a flu epidemic struck. But perhaps her most important contribution was her constant cheerful good humor.

She worked six days a week, from seven in the morning till seven at night. Often she went back to her small room so exhausted that she flopped into bed without dinner, and did not wake again until it was time to go to work. But she was happy. Because, for the first time in her life, she was needed.

On November 11, 1918, the armistice was signed. The war was over. Toronto exploded with celebration. All day long whistles blew. People ran shouting through the streets snake dancing, knocking off one anothers' hats. Young men ran around with huge dusters of flour, which they plopped over the heads of young ladies. "Hey, girlie, the war's over!"

The war was over. But the wounded were still imprisoned in their hospital beds. So Amelia stayed on at Spadina Military Hospital.

Several months after the armistice she went to the Toronto Exposition. And again she saw an airplane.

War aces, the new heroes of the hour, had taken to giving stunt exhibitions. One of them was scheduled to appear at the Toronto Exposition. Amelia and an adventurous girfriend went along to see the show. And in order not to miss a thing, the two girls stationed themselves in the center of a field.

Amelia watched, gasping with excitement, as the plane looped, spun, rolled in the air. Then the pilot must have noticed two small figures alone in the center of a clearing. He dived low, roaring straight toward them.

Amelia's friend shrieked—and ran.

But Amelia Earhart—hands on hips, feet spread—stood her ground defiantly. If something went wrong with the plane, if the pilot lost control, both he and she would be killed. But Amelia did not move.

Then, at the last possible moment, wings and struts shaking, the plane pulled out of its deafening hurtling dive.

Thrilled, exhilarated, Amelia watched it climb into the clouds. The airplane had not defeated her when she stood alone on the ground. Nor would it defeat her when she

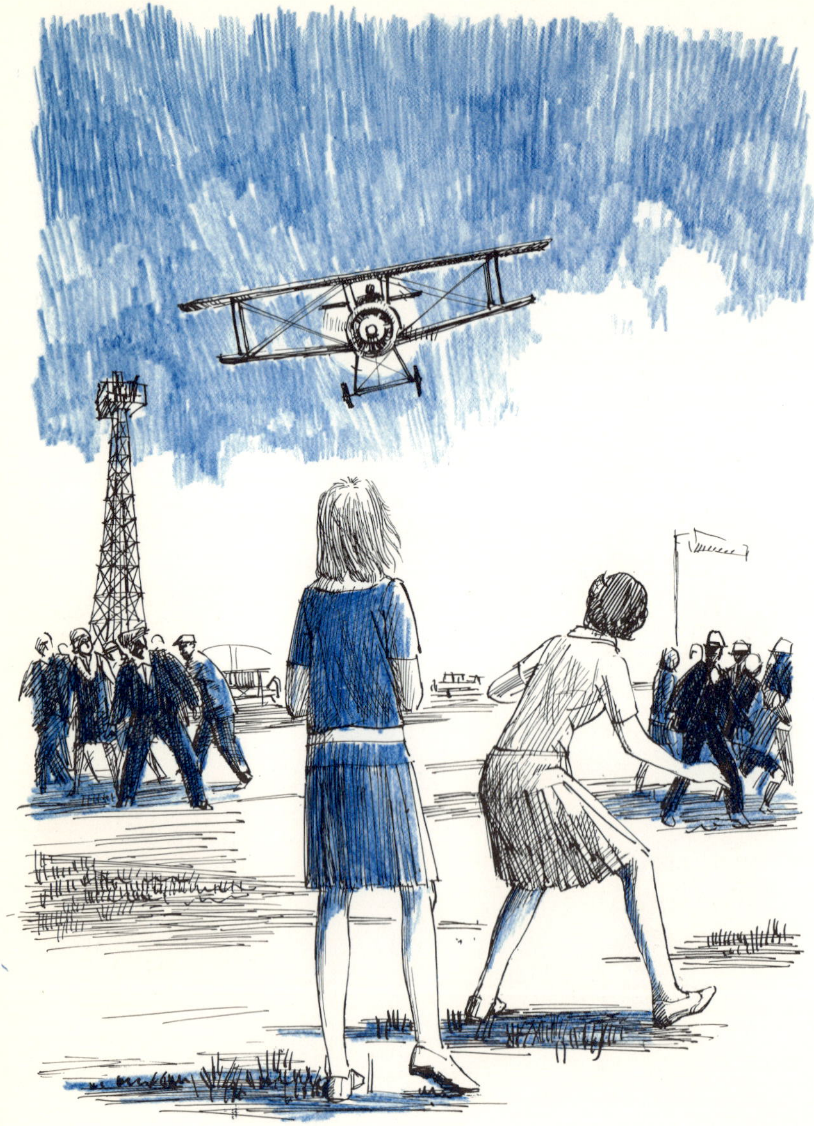

sat high in the sky! For now she was more certain than she had been of anything in her life. One day—and soon—she would learn to fly.

Amelia's career as a nurse's aide ended suddenly, when she found herself in a hospital bed. She had an abscess under her cheekbone which infected her whole system. It took months before she regained her high-spirited good health.

Then she went back to school—to Columbia University—to get her college degree.

One day she found the key to a "secret door" which led to the Columbia Library dome. And that evening she walked calmly past the library check-out desk, around to the northwest flight of stairs. Then she raced up the spiral staircase, unlocked the door, and came out onto the narrow walkway at the bottom of the dome.

She was high up, but not high enough! On her hands and knees she crawled up the smooth sides of the dome until she sat perched on the very top. She sat there for a long while, until evening deepened into night. Lights sprinkled on over the city as though the stars had fallen from the sky. A runner of moonlight shimmered on the Hudson River, and the boats, alive with tiny lights, were like fairy ships. Then, quite suddenly, moonlight caught and shimmered on the angel which topped the Cathedral of St. John the Divine.

It was the most spectacular view she had ever seen. Yet pilots high in the sky must witness worlds like this every day and night.

Suddenly she knew how and where she would spend the summer. Her parents had moved to California, where Mr. Earhart had gone into private practice. They kept writing her to join them. Well—she *would!* There were many air meets in California. Her father often mentioned them in his letters. She would go. She would learn. She would fly!

7

Her father looked at her as though she were quite mad. "Didn't you hear what I said, Amelia? It would cost a *thousand* dollars!"

Amelia laughed. "I heard, Papa. And it would take at least ten hours to learn to fly. A hundred dollars an hour. Rather expensive lessons, I agree. Still, it's what I want to do. It's what I *must* do!"

"But what *for*?" her father exploded.

"Well, just—for the fun of it," said Amelia.

They were at an air show at Dougherty Field, near Los Angeles; the sky was bright with the colors of planes flying, swooping, looping through the air.

When one of the flight officials passed by, Amelia had pushed her father toward him. "Please! Ask how much flying lessons cost."

She, too, was secretly appalled at the price. One thousand dollars! How on earth would she ever get that much money?

Suddenly drums rolled and a voice thundered through a megaphone. "Ladeeeez and gentlemen, you will now witness the most terrifying, death-defying aerial act you have ever seen!"

Amelia clutched her father's arm as they watched the tiny figure of a man crawl out along the wing of the plane which was circling high above the field. The man stood. Walked slowly, balancing, his arms outspread, to the tip of the plane. Then another plane zoomed through the sky, straight toward the first. A rope hung from its wing. The man jumped. Caught the rope. Hand over hand, he climbed, swinging in space. Then he pulled himself onto the wing of the other plane. And made his precarious way back to the cockpit.

The crowd roared. The drums rumbled. And Mr. Earhart turned to his daughter. "Amelia, you wouldn't get me up into one of those things if you *paid* me a thousand dollars!"

"Well, I'm going up!" Amelia declared. "Tomorrow! If I can't afford a lesson, at least I can pay for a *ride.*" And she ran over to the official, who booked her up for a flight the following day.

She slept very little that night. She was soaring. In imagination. And in excitement. She already felt as though she were swooping through the clouds.

The next morning when Amelia and her father arrived at the airfield, she could hardly contain herself. She kept looking at the sunny blue sky. It seemed hard to believe—in a short while she would actually be *up* there!

The pilot, a tall, slender man in a leather jacket, strode toward them. "All set to go up, sir?" he said, to Mr. Earhart.

"Not *me!*" said Mr. Earhart. "It's my daughter who's the fool of the family."

For an instant the pilot looked surprised. Then he grinned and stuck out his hand. "I'm Frank Hawkes, your pilot."

Amelia shook hands. "I'm Amelia Earhart." Her voice sounded firm, though her stomach was doing flip-flops.

Hawkes helped her climb into the open front cockpit, gave her a pair of dark goggles and a helmet. Then he signaled to another flier, who got in beside her. The two men exchanged glances, and a grin. Amelia understood. Someone had to sit beside her, to grab her if she got hysterical and tried to jump out. Well, she would show them! A girl could take a joyride quite as calmly as any man.

Frank Hawkes climbed in behind them and snapped a switch. "Contact!" he shouted. A mechanic in greasy overalls spun the propeller. And with a deafening roar and body-wracking tremble, the plane moved down the runway. Suddenly it rose into the air— heading straight toward a cluster of oil derricks to the side of the field. But it cleared the derricks and climbed into the sky.

She gasped. There, beyond the Hollywood Hills, was the Pacific Ocean. Flecks of sunlight sparked bright from the blue waters which stretched out to the far horizon.

"Altitude two thousand feet," Frank Hawkes called out. He idled the plane so that she could look around.

This was it! This was flying! This feeling of freedom, exhilaration, and joy. This was living. *This* would be her life!

Once back on the ground again she knew that she would do anything to fly—by herself.

In order to pay for lessons, she got a job as a clerk with the telephone company. Then she found herself an instructor, Neta Snook, the first woman to graduate from the Curtiss School of Aviation.

Snooky wore dirty overalls. Her freckled face was usually "made up" with airport dust and a smudge of grease. And her reddish hair was closely cropped.

"You'll have to get rid of that mop of yours," she told Amelia. "No helmet will fit properly over all that hair."

So, one day, Amelia came home with her long tawny locks cropped short.

Mrs. Earhart let out a faint shriek. "What have you *done* to yourself?"

Many people thought that a girl with bobbed hair was "shocking." Preachers often refused to let girls with short hair into church. But—aside from the shortness—the cut itself was dreadful. Mrs. Earhart wailed. "You look as though your head's been caught in a lawnmower!"

"Well," said Amelia uneasily, for she too was rather shaken by her new shorn look, "I can always grow it again."

But she never did.

At first all the flying lessons took place on the ground. Learning about the parts of the plane, the instrument panel. How to put a motor together, the principles of flight. During this period the Earharts somehow convinced themselves that their daughter would never really "go through with it." For one thing, how could she possibly afford the expensive lessons? And Mr. Earhart certainly wasn't contributing a cent to what he regarded as Amelia's Folly!

But Netta Snook was fond of her eager young student, and agreed to let Amelia pay when and as she could.

Soon they were in the air together, Amelia in the front cockpit. But the plane had dual controls. Rudder and stick were connected to a set in the rear cockpit, so that Snooky could correct any false move her student made. In addition, Snooky shouted directions and explanations. But most of her words were whipped off by the wind.

Amelia declared that she wanted to learn

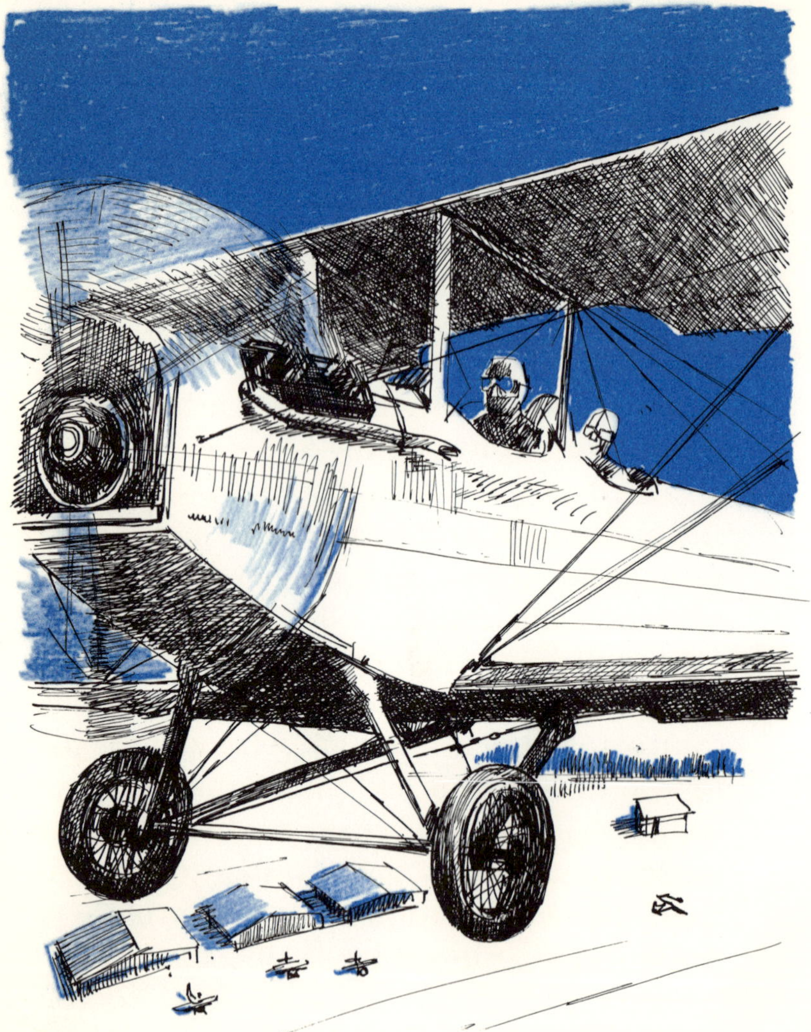

how to "stunt" before she soloed—a wise decision which was, later, to save her life many times.

Snooky turned her star student over to stunt expert, John Montijo, who gave her advance instruction on slips, stalls and spins —the three S's instead of the three R's. She learned to loop, dive, fly upside down, do sideslips and barrel rolls. The lessons went on for months, for John was less obliging—or more businesslike—than Snooky had been: No pay, no fly! And each lesson "cost" many paychecks.

But finally, the day came. John declared she was ready to go "upstairs" by herself. She would solo.

She had bought herself a brand-new patent-leather jacket, black and shiny—too shiny. She slept in it for three nights, and finished off the aging process with sandpaper. "I *look* like a pilot anyway," she assured herself when she put it on.

She did not, however, *feel* much like a

pilot as she sat, for the first time, alone in the plane. Would she remember everything? All those instruments! Instruction phrases shot through her head: *revolutions per minute of the motor . . . temperature of the oil . . . compass readings . . . keep your wings level.* How could she possibly remember it all? "Switch off. Contact," she shouted. John spun the propeller. And with a thunderous roar, the plane started taxiing across the field. Amelia made an S-turn. She was on the runway. She raced her motor. Checked each dial on the instrument panel. Pulled back on the stick and headed the nose off the ground. The plane rose into the air. But something was wrong! The left wing was sagging!

She landed, dismayed. Her instructor ran up. "Cold feet?" he yelled. She shook her head, climbed out, pointed to the wing.

One of the shock absorbers had broken. The trouble was soon fixed. But when Amelia climbed back into the cockpit again, exhilaration had been replaced by clenching fear. The plane suddenly felt so—*fragile.* There were so many things which could go wrong! And before she had even left the ground, her greatest fear was of landing.

She had heard the stories often—beginners going up alone for the first time usually took off with a whoop of joy. But when it came time to land, they developed the shakes. Many stayed up till their gas tanks were empty—simply because of the terror they felt at trying to bring the plane in for a landing. Alone.

Amelia climbed to 5,000 feet. It was a fine day. Visibility was good. As she looked around, all fear left her. It seemed she could see the whole world. Colors stood out and the shades of earth, unseen from below, formed an endless magic carpet. Trees became bushes; automobiles were flat-backed bugs; tiny dollhouses were set out in checkerboard fields.

She played around some in the plane, diving, turning, looping into figure eights. Then she dropped down for a landing. She felt in perfect control now. She was a flier. And—she suddenly decided—soon, *somehow* she would own her own plane!

But paying for flying lessons had been almost an impossibility. How could she even dream of *buying* an airplane?

She landed with a huge bump, and jounced along the dusty runway. John Montijo was the first to reach her. "That was one rotten landing!" he exclaimed as Amelia leaned out of the cockpit. But he was grinning broadly.

"How do you feel?" one of the mechanics shouted at her.

"Happy," Amelia said, speaking more to herself than to him. "Happier than I've ever been in my life."

8

She did buy a plane, a small Kinner with an air-cooled engine. The price was $2,000. Her mother helped her pay for the plane—on one condition: that Amelia stay home a bit more. The family had scarcely seen their eldest daughter for the past months, for she worked five days a week, and spent the entire weekend, it seemed, at the airfield.

Amelia took people joyriding in her Kinner. She took part in air shows. But most of all she loved to sneak away to some small secluded air field, go up, and practice. She established a new altitude record for women. And as soon as she landed, she went up again and broke her own record.

Then the infection which had downed her in Toronto flared again. It affected her sinuses. Unless it were cured, she could not fly. An operation was essential.

She sold her plane, bought a car, and she and her mother drove across the continent to Boston, where she checked in at Massachusetts General Hospital.

When she got out, cured but weak, she took courses at Harvard Summer School. By autumn she had run out of money. She must get a job—at once. Her obsession with flying had not left her. Still, one could not make a *career* of flying. No one did—except a few pilots carrying airmail. And who would hire a woman for such a job?

One morning Amelia found herself walking through a run-down section of Boston. The street was alive with the cries of children—everyone, it seemed, shouting out words in a different language. This was a section inhabited chiefly by Syrians and Chinese, with, however, an assortment of Irish, Italians, Greeks, Armenians and Russian Jews.

Denison House, one of the oldest settlement houses in the country, was down the street. Amelia walked in, asked to see the director, Miss Marion Perkins. And when she walked out she had a new job. She would be a social worker. For $15 a week.

She was even busier than she had been during her days as a hospital aide in Toronto. She was put in charge of the kindergarten. But in addition, she taught classes for older children. Sewing. Basket-making. Cooking. Dramatics. And she taught English to parents who spoke only Syrian, or Italian, or Chinese.

There were sick children to be taken to hospitals. And always more difficult, the job of trying to explain to a terrified mother who spoke no English that a hospital was

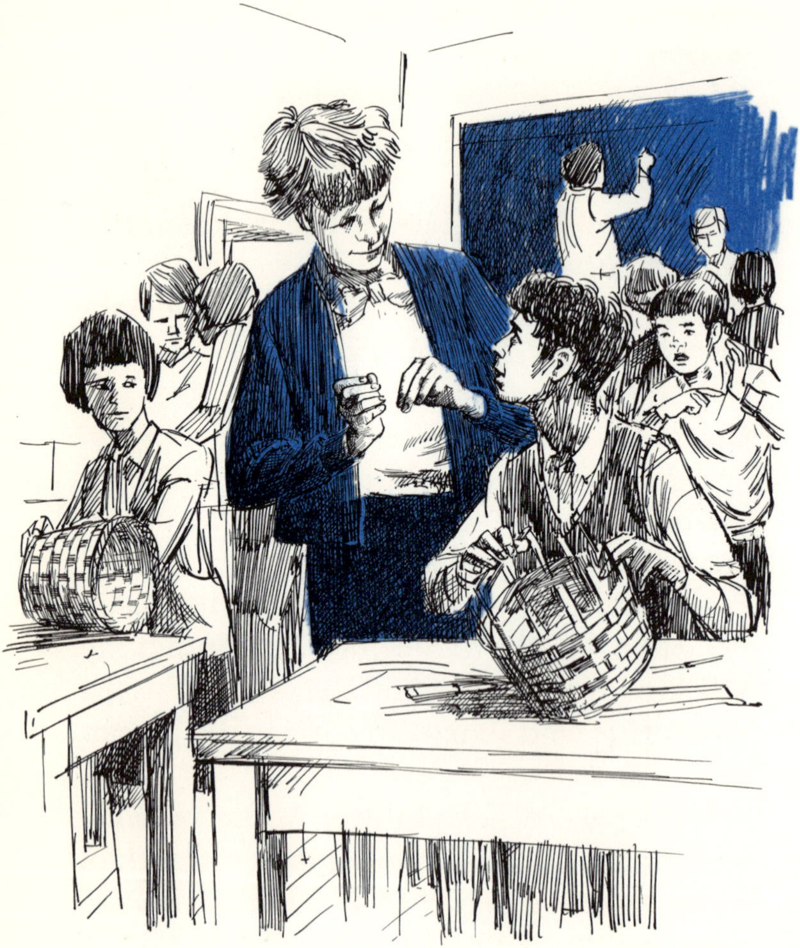

not a place where children were imprisoned, experimented on, or tortured by cruel doctors.

She loved "her children," and they reciprocated. She was often invited to their homes for dinner. Her work became so round-the-clock that she had little time left over for flying. She did, however, join the Boston chapter of the National Aeronautic Association. She came to know some of the local fliers, went up with them whenever she could. And each time she soared through the clouds, it whetted her appetite for more.

Then, on a warm April afternoon in the year 1928, Amelia Earhart was called to the telephone.

"Tell them I'm too busy to answer just now," she said to the small Chinese boy who had come to give the message.

"But he say it is velly important!" the youngster replied.

So Amelia shrugged, instructed her class

to continue with their basket weaving. And she went to the phone.

"You don't know me," a man's voice said. "My name is Railey, Captain H. H. Railey. Would you like to do something for aviation? Something which might be— dangerous."

"It depends," Amelia said. Was this a joke, a prankster? Someone organizing an aerial stunt show?

"If you're interested," Captain Railey said, "can you meet me at my office this evening?"

"Can't you tell me what this is all about?"

"Unfortunately, I can't. Not on the telephone."

There was something about his voice which suggested that this might be more than a prank, or a stunt. And Amelia agreed to meet him that evening at eight o'clock.

She sat across the desk from Captain Railey, and answered questions. About her training as a pilot. Her education. Her background. She began to feel irritated. What on earth was she being interviewed *for?*

Then, quite suddenly, he told her. "Would you fly the Atlantic?"

She looked at him. She blinked. Then she nodded. "Yes," she said. "If—"

Captain Railey grinned, and held up one hand. "There are still plenty of ifs in the whole situation. So you needn't begin with yours. Not right now. If you're interested, the first step is to come to New York City with me. There are three gentlemen who will want to interview you further."

Before she agreed to go to New York, Amelia asked some questions herself. And she learned a little at least.

The trip would be financed by a wealthy woman, Mrs. Frederick Guest—who had bought a plane, and planned to make a transatlantic flight. But because of the danger, her family insisted she must not go. She had agreed—on one condition: that some other American woman make the flight. Even though this woman would not actually pilot the plane, she must be a qualified pilot. For if the flight were successful, there would be much publicity. And Mrs. Guest wanted to show the world that women, too, were being trained to fly.

Amelia went to New York. She met the three gentlemen. One was a tall and distinguished-looking man named George Putnam, a publisher. He had been commissioned by Mrs. Guest to select the woman pilot who would make the flight. She sat in Putnam's luxurious office, trying to act cool and contained as the three men shot questions at her.

Suddenly Mr. Putnam said, "Did anyone ever tell you that you have a remarkable resemblance to Lindbergh?"

"That's true!" one of the other men exclaimed. "A lady Lindy!"

Others were interviewed. But not too many—for there were only twelve women who held pilot's licenses in all the United States.

Amelia got the job. And the chief reason for her selection was the fact that she *did* look—and act—like a female version of Charles Lindbergh, who had crashed into world headlines a year ago when he made the first solo flight across the Atlantic Ocean, and landed in Orly, France.

It was the aim of Mrs. Frederick Guest of London (formerly Amy Phipps of Pittsburgh) to do for English-American relations what Charles Lindbergh had done one year ago for French-American relations.

This beautiful, young "Lady Lindy" was, therefore, a made-to-order model for the assignment.

The plane owned by Mrs. Guest was called *The Friendship*. When Amelia saw it first, the plane was jacked up in the shadows of a hangar at East Boston. Mechanics and welders were working on the struts for pontoons which would replace the wheels. In the event—the quite likely event—that the plane landed in the ocean, wheels would be of little use. But no one knew whether pontoons would succeed in holding this heavy airship afloat.

Amelia stood staring at the plane in awe and excitement. The golden wings had a spread of 72 feet. The fusilage had been painted an orangy red. These bright hues had not been chosen for artistic effect. If they were forced to land in mid-ocean—and if ships were sent out searching for the plane—orange could be seen farther than any other color.

Amelia saw *The Friendship* only once more before the sunny Sunday morning in June, when the transatlantic flight actually got under way. Until that time she—and everyone else connected with the project—had been sworn to secrecy. Mrs. Guest did not want the press to learn of the flight in advance. If it did, she reasoned, someone else might try to enter the "race"—and *The*

Friendship would be forced to take off before full preparations had been made.

Bill Stultz had been selected to pilot the plane. He was a great pilot and navigator. He could fly by instrument. He was also an excellent radio operator. There was only one worrisome flaw. Stultz drank too much.

One other man would make the flight: a mechanic, Lou "Slim" Gordon. Slim went out to the hangar almost every day to work on the golden-winged *Friendship*. New instruments were installed and tested. There were countless trial takeoffs from Boston Bay. And at last, the plane was ready. But the weather was not.

The Friendship's backers had arranged their own personal weather bureau. Digests of British weather reports were cabled from London. More reports were radioed from ships at sea. But in Boston the days were gray and fogbound. When the weather cleared in Boston, it was rough in the mid-Atlantic. When the Atlantic was favorable, a sultry calm sat over Boston Harbor, making it impossible for the heavy plane to get into the air.

Finally, however, on June 3, 1928, the fog was not too thick in the harbor and a brisk wind blew in from the southeast. Amelia, Stultz and Slim Gordon climbed into the waiting tugboat. When they reached the plane, Slim took the tarpaulin covers off the three motors. Bill checked the radio, the instruments. Slim cranked the motors, then climbed into the copilot's seat. The plane taxied down the harbor, propellers whirring.

Then, suddenly, smoothly, *The Friendship* lifted into the air. They were actually off!

9

A few minutes later a sudden icy blast shot into the plane. Amelia turned—and gasped. The cabin door was open! The spring lock had broken off. Slim came back to see what could be done about it—and very nearly tumbled out the gaping doorway.

He managed to tie a string through a leather thong in the door. This he anchored to a heavy gasoline can. "That should do it," he said, and returned to the controls.

Amelia squatted on the floor, her eyes

uneasily on the door. She saw the gasoline can start to move, dived toward it. The door again slid open. She almost fell out, headfirst. The Atlantic Ocean glinted far below.

This time Slim tied the cord to a brace inside the cabin.

Amelia, slightly shaken, squatted between two gasoline tanks and started writing in her logbook. An eventful beginning. Not five minutes out of Boston Harbor and already they had very nearly lost two members of their crew.

Several hours later she noted in her logbook: "Hooray! Nova Scotia at 8:55. . . . Many white gulls flying over green land. A few houses clustered together. . . . There is a rocky ledge around the islands which makes a ruffle. . . . Our shadow skims over the treetops. . . ."

They landed in Halifax Harbor to take on extra gasoline. But when they started off again, they discovered that one of the primers had broken. Should they stop and solder it? Or try to reach Trepassy, where more fuel would be taken on? Trepassy—the takeoff point across the Atlantic Ocean!

They'd already lost an hour with the time change. They decided to press on.

But they didn't get far. Thick fog spread out around them. *Like a great fuzz,* Amelia noted in her log book. Rain slashed against the windows. Suddenly Bill announced, "Look, the Newfoundland coast is bad enough on a sunny day. No use to try it when we're flying blind." So they turned back.

By now the "secret flight" had made headlines. It had been announced in Boston that three aviators were off to fly the Atlantic. But what had *not* been announced was that one of the three was an aviatrix.

Consequently, Amelia was virtually smuggled off the plane and into her room in a small hotel in Dartmouth. At midnight, as she lay in bed, she thanked her particular stars that her presence was unknown—for she could hear reporters knocking at the door of Bill and Slim's room, pleading with the pilots to get up and dress for an interview and pictures.

But when the trio came down to breakfast—at six o'clock the next morning— Amelia was "discovered" by reporters and photographers. A few hours later her name was in headlines. AMELIA EARHART: LADY LINDY.

Publicity preceded the flight. And because

of it, the landing at Trepassy that morning turned into an hilarious rodeo—at sea. There were a dozen launches waiting to greet them in the bay. Each had its "maritime cowboy" with a rope, trying to lasso the plane, and pull it in to a mooring.

Slim climbed out onto a pontoon, yelled frantically at the boats—trying to ward them off. Rope could break a propeller. Or one of the welcomers might get too close to the whirling props—and be killed. Suddenly Slim himself was lassoed, almost fell into the water.

Bill sat in the cockpit, cursing. Amelia was doubled up with laughter.

Finally, a cameraman from Paramount realized that the plane was capable of making its own way to a mooring. And he succeeded in clearing a path for *The Friendship*.

The following thirteen days were grim. First, a howling gale kept the trio stranded in the small hamlet on the coast of Norman's Woe—an appropriately named place, Amelia decided.

The storm finally stopped. But the raging northwest wind kept up for days. And Trepassy Harbor was too narrow for takeoff with a heavy load—unless the wind blew from the right direction.

Then Slim discovered a crack in the oil tanks—which he mended with cement and adhesive tape. The radio cut out—a loose connection. Bill fixed it—or thought he did. The left motor needed repair. Then the pontoons. It seemed that the plane would fall to pieces before they ever got out of this place!

But the most torturing problem of all concerned Bill Stultz. In the air, Amelia knew, he was a great pilot. But on the ground—especially when caught in the mire of inactivity—he turned to drink.

Amelia spent many sleepless hours wondering whether to cable George Putnam and ask that he replace Stultz with another pilot. She resolved finally to try her best to "keep Stultz in shape," so that when the time came to take off—if it ever did—he would be ready.

The time came finally on a Sunday morning, June 17. The wind in the harbor was reasonably right. The weather reports telegraphed from New York were also favorable. But the pilot, Bill Stultz, was far from "in shape."

When he taxied *The Friendship* madly downwind, he was going much too fast. The plane rocked and staggered. But somehow it climbed into the air. They were on their way.

Amelia—clenching her fists, holding her breath—felt none of the exhilaration which had filled her when they had taken off from Boston Harbor. Instead, terror swept through her.

A week ago—after four futile attempts to get into the air—they had stripped the plane of everything possible in order to lighten the load. The rubber life raft. The life preservers. A motion-picture camera. Coats. Cushions. But the plane had still been too heavy to take off in the narrow harbor. There was only one more way to lighten the load. Dump the extra gasoline.

They had done so. Unloaded 300 pounds of gas. This meant they had just enough fuel on board to make the trip. But if a storm blew them out of the way . . . If the pilot lost his course . . . If they found themselves circling aimlessly for even a half hour, they would run out of gas. They would crash.

Their lives depended on Bill Stultz' flying ability. And Bill was obviously in no condition to fly!

One engine was spluttering from the dousing of sea spray on takeoff. Then they headed into thick fog. They climbed higher—to be caught and buffeted by a sudden snowstorm. The plane shook violently.

Bill pointed the nose down. They bucked a fierce headwind. Dashing rain dripped in through the windows. They lurched into violent downdrafts and updrafts. Then the plane upended, hurtled into a steep dive.

A whiskey bottle rolled across the cabin floor, a bottle Bill Stultz must have hidden when he came on board!

Amelia grabbed it. Should she throw it out? What if Stultz came back looking for his bottle—and it was gone? Would he claim he *had* to have a drink? Would he go to pieces? But what if he *found* the bottle? Could he pilot the plane dead drunk—keep it on course?

Could *she* take over? She knew without doubt that she lacked the experience to maneuver three tons of aircraft through the storms which raged above the Atlantic Ocean.

She clung to the forward bulkhead, the bottle in one hand, praying that the plane would right itself, that they would climb somehow into clear, smooth skies.

Pilot Bill Stultz never came back to find that bottle. He sat at the controls all that day. And all through the night. "He flies as if he were part of the plane," Amelia wrote in her logbook. "He has the instincts of a homing pigeon."

It was fortunate that he did, for at eight o'clock that night Slim called out, "The radio isn't working!"

They were cut off—in the clouds. They could no longer check their position with passing ships. They could not signal if they needed help.

Perhaps, when they flew into the darkness of night, they could check their position by the stars.

And they did, finally, see the stars. But not for long—for storm clouds again enfolded the plane in blackness. Through the endless-seeming night Amelia sat cramped between the gas tanks, making entries in her logbook in the dark. The cabin was freezing. She put on the huge fur-lined flying suit which a friend had lent her. But even this did not keep her warm.

Around three in the morning she wrote: "The mass of soggy cloud we came through is pink with dawn." They were still flying blind. But at least, now, they could begin to see one another!

She moved over to her "daytime place" by the small window and knelt, staring out. After a time, the clouds broke. She saw the sea. And then—"A ship!" she cried out. "Look!"

A ship. But why was it cutting *across* their

path? Were they flying off course? Were they heading out to sea? Or were they flying parallel to land, without knowing it?

"We've got to find out," Bill Stultz said grimly. "We have less then two hours' gas left!"

Hastily Amelia wrote a message asking that the ship paint bearings on the deck so that they could tell where they were. She put the note into a bag with a few oranges for ballast. Bill circled as she dropped the bag through the hatchway in the bottom of the plane. But it landed in the water, far from the ship.

They circled the ship again and again. Dropped more messages. None of them landed.

"If we come down beside her," Bill said, "we can probably land safely. Be hauled aboard. But of course that would mean we'd have failed in our mission."

No one said anything. It was thus agreed they would go on.

At eight-fifty in the morning they saw another ship. Amelia wrote in her logbook: "Trans steamer. Try to get bearing. Radio won't respond to Stultz's frantic calls. One hour's gas. Mess. All craft cutting our course. Why?"

Should they circle *this* ship? Try to land another message? But they had no gas to waste. They kept on—flying by instrument. And by instinct.

Their fuel supply would last but another half hour. They were flying low. Five hundred feet. They should have been passing over Ireland. But they saw nothing except bleak gray sea. The gasoline in the tanks was vanishing fast.

Ahead, more clouds—low, dark. They looked almost solid.

They *were* solid!

Slim had been eating a ham sandwich. With a yell he threw it out the window. "Land!" he shouted.

Bill said nothing. But he was smiling.
Amelia closed her eyes in silent wordless thanks.

With the little gas left, they cruised along the coast of what they hoped was England. Trying to find a harbor, Bill circled what looked like a factory town. Then brought the plane down in the channel.
Amelia Earhart looked at her watch. "Well," she remarked quite coolly, "the trip took us exactly twenty hours and forty minutes." But her words were drowned by the roaring of the motors.

10

"But it's *you* they want to see again, miss," said the wife of the factory foreman. "So go on to the balcony like a good girl and let them have another look at you."

"They don't understand!" Amelia protested. "I was only a passenger. I did nothing but—sit there. Like a sack of potatoes."

"Never mind who steered the plane, miss. *You're* the first woman in all history to fly across the Atlantic Ocean!"

They were sitting in a factory office of the

Frickers Metal Company in Burry Port, Wales. They had landed less than an hour ago, yet already crowds and newspapermen had gathered.

Once again the trio of pilots went onto the balcony to wave and smile at the crowd. Once again it was the slim girl in the brown riding breeches and white silk blouse who drew the wildest cheers.

And it remained that way through all the unbelievable days they spent in England. Amelia stayed in London with Mrs. Guest, the short, compact and friendly woman who had sponsored the flight. Invitations poured in. Everyone wanted to meet the girl who had, overnight, become the darling of the Western world. Parties were given in her honor by lords and ladies, mayors, and officials of the Air League of the British Empire. She attended the Tattoo at Aldershot where Royal Air Force planes performed in the searchlight-streaked night sky. She visited the Embassy Club—and danced again and again with His Royal Highness the Prince of Wales.

Her lovely smiling face was featured daily in the British newspapers. Letters and telegrams of congratulations piled up like snowdrifts. One of the telegrams came from President Coolidge. And she answered it in the same way she tried to answer all the congratulations and acclaim: "SUCCESS ENTIRELY DUE GREAT SKILL OF MR. STULTZ. . . ."

But the more she tried to disclaim her sudden fame, the more she was acclaimed for her delightful modesty.

Two weeks later Amelia, Stultz and Slim Gordon sailed for the United States.

Amelia spent much of the trip walking the deck, deep in thought. She had been warned that the American public would give her the same acclaim she had won in England. Only more so. Parties. Receptions. Interviews. Ticker tape parades. Again she'd be made a heroine—a false heroine, she felt. For only the accident of being a woman had shot her into the world spotlight. She herself had done nothing.

But she need not *remain* a false heroine!

Silently, on the steamship trip back to the States, she made a resolution. She would give up social work. She would devote her life from now on to aviation. And one day she would be worthy of the acclaim she had already won.

One day she, Amelia M. Earhart, would become the first woman pilot to fly the Atlantic Ocean—alone.

England, it turned out, *was* a mere dress rehearsal to what awaited Amelia Earhart at home. As their ship sailed up the Hudson, sirens shrieked, fireboats sprayed jubilant streams of water, bands played. And during the days ahead, her every move was enthusiastically recorded by newspaper reporters; what she wore, every chance remark, even what she ate for breakfast.

Never, Amelia felt, had anyone won so

much praise for doing so little—which only strengthened her resolve to "fulfill" her fame.

G. P. Putnam—in addition to asking her out numerous times—also asked her to write her account of the Atlantic flight. She did. It was called *Forty Hours, Twenty Minutes.*

There were hundreds of speaking invitations. She accepted as many as she could. Manufacturers asked her to endorse their products. She did. And within the first few months she earned more than $50,000. The plans she had in mind would cost money. The plane she wanted to buy would cost money. Now she had the money.

She knew that she needed a great deal more experience in the air. So she set out on a cross-country flight. She would "gypsy" her way across the United States, stopping whenever and wherever she wished—or had to.

In Pittsburgh her plane hit a ditch in landing, turned upside down. Amelia emerged unhurt. But newspaper headlines announced: AMELIA EARHART NEAR DEATH IN CRASH.

In Hobbs, New Mexico, she made a forced landing in the middle of Main Street. Startled citizens gathered around the plane. They were amazed to see a woman climb out—a strange-looking woman. Her face was sunburned red. But when she took off her goggles, her eyes were surrounded by huge white circles. She looked like an owl—and, appropriately, she walked into the Owl Café for fried eggs, bread and milk.

In Pecos, Texas, she had tire trouble upon landing. Four thousand feet above El Paso she had engine trouble, made another forced landing. High above Utah she again ran into engine trouble.

She returned home in the autumn of 1928, the first woman who had ever flown alone across the continent, and back again.

Job offers poured in. Many of them had nothing to do with flying. She accepted the position of aviation editor on *Cosmopolitan* magazine. In presenting her to the readers, editor O. O. McIntyre wrote: "Amelia has become a symbol of a new womanhood—a symbol, I predict, that will be emulously patterned after by thousands of young girls in their quest for the Ideal."

He was right. Amelia even looked the part. Her slender boyish figure, her short bob, her long youthful waist exactly duplicated the fashion figure "in vogue" at the time. And her career fulfilled the dreams of every woman who longed for "female emancipation."

She then helped to organize an airline: Transcontinental Air Transport, and she became a vice-president.

And in February, 1931, America's "Ideal Girl" fulfilled her image completely. She married George Palmer Putnam, the handsome, charming, wealthy and powerful publisher—the man who had originally helped select her for *The Friendship* flight.

Would marriage mean that the world heard little more about AE (as everyone—including her own husband—now called her)?

Hardly. Three months later she became the first pilot to make a cross-country flight in an autogiro. On the return trip her husband, GP, went to Detroit to meet her. He watched the giro spin down from the skies, clatter above the treetops.

There was a terrible crash. The autogiro lay split apart in a cloud of smoke. GP raced toward the wreck. He ran into one of the support wires, flew up, over, landed flat on his back.

Amelia walked away from the crack-up unhurt. She saw her husband, hurried over to him. He did not seem to be hurt, so she knelt beside him with a grin. "You see," she announced, "flying *is* safest after all. If you'd been with me, you wouldn't have been hurt!"

GP nodded, turned to get up. And winced in pain. In *his* landing he had cracked three ribs!

11

Something was up. But no one knew what—except AE, GP, and two airplane mechanics.

At last the weather reports were good!

Amelia was at the Putnams' country home in Rye, New York. She left suddenly without lunch. Drove, racing, to the airfield. Landed three and a half hours later at St. John, New Brunswick. Reached Harbour Grace in Newfoundland the following afternoon. The plane—her Lockheed Vega—was waiting and ready. And at twelve minutes after seven that evening, Amelia Earhart was heading out to sea.

The date was May 20, 1932—five years to the day after Charles A. Lindbergh had set out on the first solo flight across the Atlantic.

Amelia was out to make another world record: the first *woman* to fly across the Atlantic—alone.

At first the flight seemed a dream coming true. The view was vast and lovely. As she looked about, she felt she was gulping beauty. The clouds were marvelous shapes in white, some trailing shimmering veils. In the distance the highest peaks of the fog mountains were tinted pink with the setting sun.

Gradually she flew into darkness, star-flecked, with moonlight shimmering through the endless skies.

Then, suddenly, the dream turned into nightmare. Something happened that had never occurred in all her twelve years of flying. The dials of the altimeter started to spin crazily. She could no longer tell how high she was above the sea. And she was flying through thick darkness—flying into a storm.

Rain hit against the windshield like handfuls of gravel. Lightning whipped and cracked across the nose of the plane. The Vega was shaking in the fierce wind; then the plane started bucking like a wild horse. How far above the ocean was she? Would the downdrafts shove her too far toward the water—so that she would be unable to rise again?

For an hour she fought the plane through the storm. If she could only rise high enough, fly above the treacherous clouds.

She climbed—for thirty minutes. Climbed into still further danger. Ice collected on the wings. Then the dials on the tachometer began to spin wildly. It was icebound! The dial on the rate-of-climb indicator fell off. The stick and rudder became sloppy and unresponsive.

Then one wing lurched up, snapped over. Heavy with ice, the plane spun, over and over—out of control—straight down through the darkness, through the wild storm, toward the ocean.

With all her strength, Amelia drove the stick all the way forward. Somehow she brought the plane into control, nosed it up out of the perilous dive.

Her heart thumping with terror, she looked down. Moonlight lit the waves. She was a dangerous 100 feet above the water.

The warmth of the lower atmosphere melted the ice off the wings of the plane. But then clouds and fog covered the ocean. Without the altimeter she could not risk flying too low—over waves which she could not see. Yet she did not want to fly up again into the raging storm.

A snake of flame lashed out from the engine. What was it? She suspected a broken weld in the manifold ring. If it burned through, the ship was doomed.

She was 600 miles from Newfoundland. But 1,400 miles from her destination. Yet how could she go back? With no altimeter she could never land at Harbour Grace in the dark. She must go on. The orange flames licked evilly against the black night.

She flew on, trying not to watch the fire, praying that the metal weld was strong enough to hold through the hours ahead. But the flame was roaring angrily. The weakening metal began vibrating. Shaking, like a skeleton's bones.

Finally, she flew into the first streaks of dawn. She turned on the reserve tanks—and saw she had a leaky gauge!

She *must* come down. Perhaps she was near the tip of Ireland. She turned northeast.

Low, hanging thunderclouds. And beneath them—

She slumped over her controls in unbelieving relief.

Mountains!

But where to land on this rocky coast?

A tiny railroad, its bars silver in the sunlight. It might lead to an airfield.

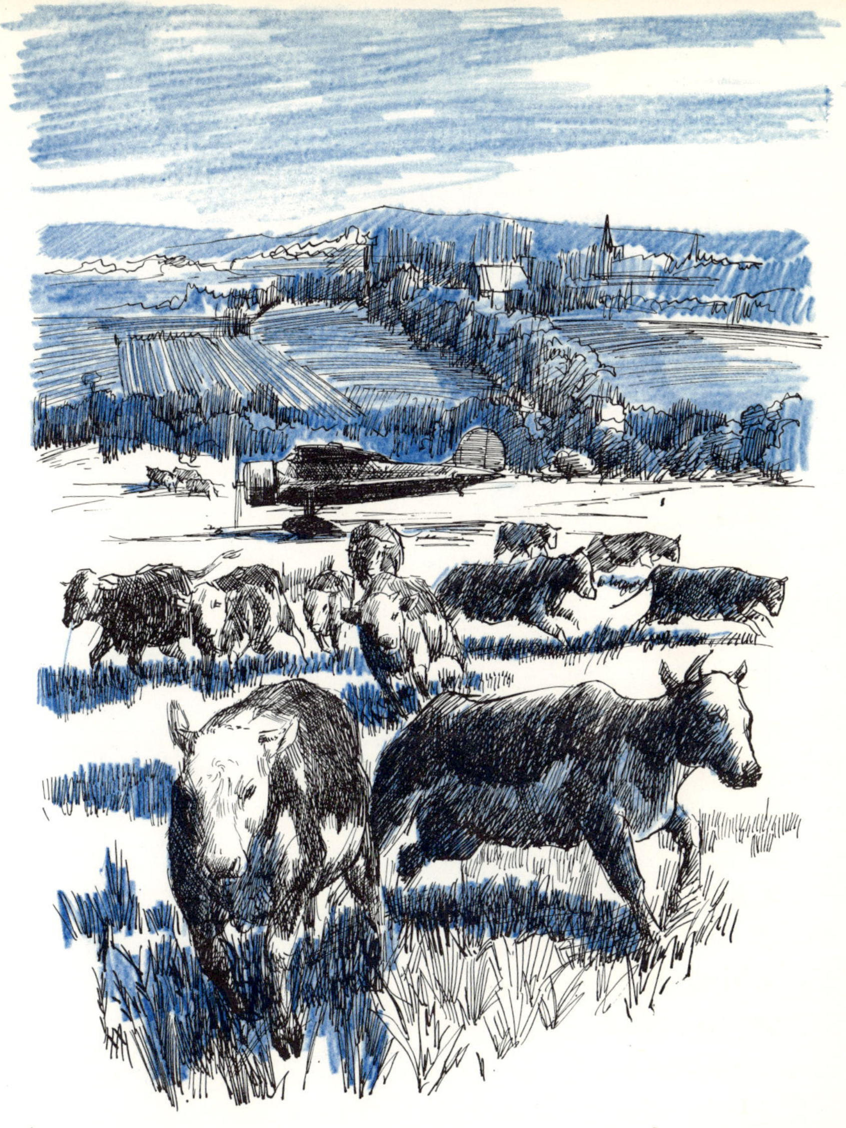

At last! A space of flat green. As she landed her Lockheed in a field, frightened cows loped out of the way.

She had set her plane down in an Irish pasture, near Londonderry. The flight had taken fourteen hours and fifty-six minutes—the longest minutes in Amelia's life.

"My chances," she later wrote, "were one in ten of ever making it. Five hours of storm during black midnight, when I kept right side up by instrument alone, buffeted about as I never was before.

"After the fire broke out I kept wondering in a detached way whether one would prefer drowning to being burned alive."

Because she had flown so close to death for so many hours, she welcomed the new explosion of fame and adulation which followed her successful Atlantic solo. Joyously, she entered into "the fun of it."

She'd brought nothing with her but a toothbrush and her flying clothes, so she went on the first real shopping spree of her life.

And she needed the lovely clothes, for there were more invitations to parties and receptions than anyone could attend in a lifetime.

There were also thousands of letters, telegrams, cables of congratulations. One came from the President of the United States inviting her to the White House; another from the King and Queen of Belgium, inviting her to the Royal Palace for luncheon; another from Brtain's King George. There was also a cable from her dry cleaner in Rye, New York: *"I knew you'd make it. I never lost a customer."*

Finally, after some three weeks of parties, receptions, awards and acclaim in London, Paris, Rome and Belgium, Amelia and her husband sailed home on the *Ile de France.*

Now that she had set a new world record, would Amelia Earhart "retire," become Mrs. George Palmer Putnam?

Not likely.

She continued setting records.

The first person—not *woman* this time—

but the first pilot to fly alone from Honolulu to California. Twenty four hundred miles nonstop over the Pacific Ocean.

The first person to fly nonstop from Mexico City to New York City (or, Newark Airport). Two thousand one hundred twenty-five miles.

She wrote another book: *The Fun of It*. And she taught at Purdue University in Lafayette, Indiana. Her assignment was to teach the girls something about aviation, and jobs related to it. But in fact, she taught them far more than that.

She believed that women should have the same opportunities as men in *developing* their abilities. And then, that they should be given the same opportunities as men to *use* their abilities. She was against the "employment office classifications" for jobs: this for women, that for men.

She inspired and encouraged "her girls" to study for careers they undoubtedly would not have dared to try—were it not for the example of their "idol": AE.

But Purdue University also did something for AE. Without her knowing a word about it, they raised a fund: the Amelia Earhart Fund. It came to $50,000. "With *this*," the president of Purdue told AE on presentation day, "you ought to be able to buy the kind of airplane you want!"

Fifty thousand dollars to buy a plane! The kind of plane she had dreamed about! The plane which was able to make the flight she had dreamed about—a flight around the world!

12

"But *why*, Amelia?" her husband protested. "It's just too dangerous."

"Why?" She answered with the smile he knew so well, and loved so much. "Because I want to."

No man had ever attempted it, not even Charles Lindbergh. To fly around the world taking the longest possible route, at the equator.

"But I promise you, GP"—she was serious

now—"after I come back from this one, I'll settle down. At least," she added, with her grin, "there won't be any more really long-distance flights. I feel I've got just one more long flight left in me. And this is it."

Her husband stood by her, helped her. But her goal remained a secret. When Amelia spent her Purdue check on a two-motor, red-winged Lockheed Electra, only she and he knew where this plane was headed.

They took off from Oakland California on the afternoon of March 17, 1937: Amelia and three navigators. (She planned to navigate at night by sun and stars as well as instrument, and it was difficult to take careful reckonings and fly at the same time.)

It was St. Patrick's Day, and AE pinned an Irish shamrock to her shirt for good luck.

Her luck held through the long night, and she brought the plane to a safe landing as sunrise spread soft colors through the Hawaiian skies.

They dropped one of the navigators, according to plan, at Honolulu. And, according to plan, they took off two days later bound for the second lap of the round-the-world-trip: tiny Howland Island in the South Pacific.

The motors roared. The plane moved easily down the runway. It was about to lift off the ground, when suddenly the plane lurched. A wing crashed, then crumpled against the concrete runway. The plane turned over; its landing gear flew through the air.

A scream rose from the crowd which had gathered to watch the takeoff. Sirens shrieked. An ambulance sped across the field. A streak of flame shot up from the broken plane.

A few minutes later AE and her two navigators walked away from the wreck, unhurt.

Instantly, they were surrounded by reporters who had gathered to watch the takeoff—for the "secret flight" had by now made world headlines. "Of course," one of the reporters exclaimed, "you'll give up the trip now?"

"I think not," Amelia said.

If she could afford the tremendous costs involved in repairing the plane, she would try again.

The plane took several months—and considerable money—to be made ready. "I more-or-less mortgaged the future," Amelia wrote. "But without regret, for what are futures for?"

June 1 was set as the new takeoff date. But the weather over Africa was often rough in late June, so Amelia decided to fly west this time, completing the African part of her journey before the storms came.

She flew her plane across the continent from Oakland, California, to Miami. And, on June 1, as dawn streaked the skies above Miami Airport, Amelia and her husband sat close together on the cold concrete steps of the hangar building. They were holding hands. They did not speak. There was too much to say.

Death had never come so close as it had during the last crash in Hawaii. Was this a warning? Amelia did not believe in prophecies. Facing her was the most difficult and perilous flight any pilot had ever attempted. She had excuse enough to withdraw now. But from the moment she had walked away from the wrecked plane in Hawaii, her decision had been to go on.

A mechanic was resoldering a broken thermocouple on the plane. When he called out that everything was ready, Amelia stood up. "Her eyes," GP later wrote, "were clear with the light of the adventure that lay ahead."

The first stop was Puerto Rico. As they approached the island, a fishing pole with a note tied to it appeared over her left shoulder: a note informing her that she was flying off course, too far south.
She turned, and grinned at her navigator, Fred Noonan.
She had selected Noonan for very sound reasons. Not only was he known as one of the best navigators in the business, but he had flown the Pacific seventeen times. For five years Noonan had worked as a navigator for Pan American, the airline which had—two years ago—opened the first airmail service from San Francisco to Manila, via Honolulu, Midway Island, Wake and Guam. Then, in October 1936, Pan Am had pioneered transpacific passenger flights on that route. Fred Noonan knew the Pacific, and the skies

above it perhaps better than any other navigator. He knew how to find a tiny island surrounded by thousands of miles of empty ocean.

Noonan had another specialty as well. Pan Am was also the first American airline to operate in South America, and as navigator on many of these flights Fred Noonan knew the perils and the possibilities of flying over a land of dense jungles and craggy mountains.

In addition, Amelia was certain that the lanky, soft-spoken, easygoing Fred Noonan would make an ideal flying companion.

The next morning they took off from San Juan Airport for the 3,000-mile stretch along the coast of South America to Natal—the takeoff spot for their flight across the Atlantic to Africa. In all those 3,000 miles there were only four airfields worthy of the name. If they were forced to land anywhere in between, they would, in all likelihood, have to come down in dense jungle, or in the ocean.

But thanks in the main to Noonan's skilled navigation, they made their way through mountainous rain clouds and dangerous head winds to Paramaribo Airport.

Amelia had expected a hacked-out clearing. Instead, she found one of the best airports she had ever seen. The next airport—Fortaleza—was also suprisingly excellent. And when Pan Am put all its facilities at her disposal, Amelia decided to have the plane readied there for the South Atlantic trip to Africa.

While mechanics worked on the plane, Amelia turned tourist. She explored the crowded streets of Fortaleza, one of Brazil's largest cities. She took photos of burros ladened with produce—and small boys. Women carrying the morning shopping on their heads. Fishermen setting sail in their *jangadas*—sailboats made of logs bound into a raft.

Two nights later, at 3:15 a.m. they took off in the windy darkness from Natal. Bound for Africa. The land of Amelia's childhood dreams and fantasies. She remembered the games of maptraveling they had played, sitting in the old carriage in Grandpa's barn. The romantic and mysterious-sounding African names. Many of them were now on her itinerary. Dakar. Gao. El Fasher. Khartoum on the banks of the Nile. Massawa. Assab on the Red Sea. In a matter of hours she would actually *be* in all these places!

13

In a matter of hours she had been—and departed. The flashes she saw of Africa were fascinating. But too fast. "Kaleidoscopic first impressions," Amelia wrote. "An amusing, friendly riot of bright raiment adorning good-natured ebony people. Their clothing contrasted gaudily with the neutral background of brown plains, bare hills, parched vegetation and drab dwellings."

One day she would return with GP. Return and really "see" Africa. But now she was attempting to set a world record. Now the motto of every moment was "push on!"

A few days later she landed in Karachi, the first pilot to make a nonstop flight across the Red Sea to India. There, while her plane was being serviced, she took a camel ride.

"It was a startling take-off," she wrote. "As a camel's hind legs unfold, you are threatened with a nose-dive forward. Then with a lurch that can unhorse (I mean uncamel) the unwary, the animal's center section, so to speak, hoists into the air. It is reminiscent of the first symptoms of a flat spin. Fred shouted out, "Better wear your parachute!"

Two days later they were on their way to Calcutta. First they were hit and buffeted by a swirling sandstorm. Then the plane was attacked by large black eagles. If one of them dived into the propellers, it would be chopped to bits—which would choke the engines. The plane would crash.

She escaped the eagles—and met an even more dangerous enemy: the monsoons.

They began on the night of June 17, as Amelia and Fred slept, exhausted, in Calcutta.

By dawn the runway at Dumdum Airport was soaking wet. It was dangerous to take off in the sticky mud. But more heavy rain was coming. If they waited, they might not be able to leave until the monsoon season ended in September.

The spinning wheels finally lifted and the plane just managed to clear the fringe of trees at the airport's edge. They traveled low over endless rice paddies and dense jungle to Akyab, town of the golden pagodas. Then on to Rangoon and into the wildest weather Amelia had ever met.

When they finally landed, they were driven in style to the home of the American consul. There, before she fell asleep, Amelia—as usual—made notes for the book she would write when she returned home.

The book to be called: *World Flight.* At each stop she mailed her notes home to her husband.

She sat now beneath the mosquito netting in the large and luxurious bed, trying to capture in words the weather she had just fought through:

"The wind, dead ahead, began to whip furiously. Relentless rain pelted us. The monsoon, I find, lets down more liquid per second than I thought could come out of the skies; rain so savage that it beat off patches of paint along the plane's wings. . . . An almost unbroken wall of water which would have drowned us had our cockpit not been secure."

They did not escape the dreaded monsoons until they had left the fairy-tale city of Bangkok with its gilded spires and many-colored tile roofs glinting in the sudden sunshine.

Then over the Gulf of Siam to Singapore.

"I felt as if I were dreaming," Amelia wrote, "to be flying over such fabulous waters, with the shores of Siam on the right and Cambodia on the left. . . . Then as we crossed the Malay peninsula to Alor Star, there looked up from the charts stretched out on my knees marvelous names like Bang Taphang, Lem Tane, Koh Phratnog.

"The sea, really mauve, melted into a blue sky with companies of little white clouds marching through it. A fairer day could not have been."

The fair weather held through Singapore ("when I shut off the plane's engines at landing, music from a near-by Chinese theater floated up to greet us"). . . .

To Java . . . "A thousand tiny islets cluster along the Javanese coast. Some are covered with a heavy growth of palms that crowd down to the water's edge. Others are outlined with narrow ribbons of beach, separating the deeper green of their verdure from the exquisite turquoise tones that mark the surrounding shallow water. The white sails of tiny fishing craft flashed in the sunlight. . . . What with all that lovely world to look at, it required concentration for a pilot to attend to her knitting, which is to say, her horizon and her instruments."

On June 30, Amelia made the long flight from Port Darwin, Australia, to Lae, New Guinea. She was exhausted. She had traveled over five continents, crossed the equator four times, flown 22,000 miles in forty days.

She was looking forward now to returning home. She wanted to get back to the States by the Fourth of July. And, on July 24, she would celebrate a very special birthday with GP. She would be thirty-nine years old. *High time to give up long-distance flying*, she reflected, a little ruefully.

Ahead of her lay the longest leg of the world flight—and the most dangerous. She would fly across 2,556 miles of Pacific Ocean to tiny Howland Island, a sandy knoll barely a mile and a half long, and a half mile wide. No one had ever tried to make this flight before. And with good reason. If one of the navigation instruments were off even a hair's breadth, they would miss the island, which, from the air, was only a tiny speck of land surrounded by 7,000 miles of ocean.

Yet Howland was the only land directly on the route between New Guinea and Hawaii—Hawaii, the final stop before the return to Oakland, California, where her husband would be waiting.

At Howland, as at all the stops en route, there were huge containers of gasoline marked AMELIA EARHART. These fuel tanks were part—the most important part—of the months of preparation AE and GP had put in before the world flight.

At ten o'clock on the morning of July 2, 1937, Amelia Earhart's silver-winged Electra roared down the runway—a long strip cut out of the jungle and ending in a steep cliff above the sea.

The plane, with AE at the controls, headed up into the clouds.

The U.S. Coast Guard cutter *Itasca* lay anchored off Howland Island. The ship was to give Amelia regular radio bearings. Throughout the long day and the following night they tried to make contact with the plane. Several times they succeeded.

At 2:45 A.M. Amelia reported that the weather was "cloudy and overcast." Did that mean Fred Noonan was not able to use the stars for celestial navigation?

At 7:42 in the morning Amelia's voice came in loud and clear, but high and frantic. "We must be on you. But cannot see you. Gas is running low. Been unable to reach you by radio. We are flying at altitude 1,000 feet."

The *Itasca* answered, kept answering.

At 7:58 Amelia's voice came again. "We are circling, but cannot hear you!"

She had been in the air for twenty hours. She should have reached Howland Island within eighteen hours of flying.

At 8:45 her voice came once more, broken and frenzied, giving her position.

That was Amelia Earhart's last message. She was never heard from again.

Back home GP and Fred Noonan's bride of one month were notified: the plane was lost. But a search was already on for the missing fliers.

The *Itasca,* a battleship, four destroyers, a minesweeper, an aircraft carrier and all its planes searched the area for sixteen days.

George Putnam refused to give up hope. "IF THEY ARE DOWN," he wired from San Francisco, "THEY CAN STAY AFLOAT INDEFINITELY. THEIR EMPTY TANKS WILL GIVE THEM BOUYANCY. BESIDES, THEY HAVE ALL THE EMERGENCY EQUIPMENT THEY'LL NEED— EVERYTHING."

But Fred Noonan and Amelia Earhart were never found.

For weeks after her disappearance Amelia's letters and pages from her logbook kept on coming home to her husband, with postmarks from her stopoff spots around the world. He published them all in a book: a book which was to be called *World Flight* by Amelia Earhart. It had a new title. It was called *Last Flight*.

The last words in that book were those she wrote the evening before she took off for Howland Island:

"Not much more than a month ago I was on the other shore of the Pacific, looking westward. This evening, I looked eastward over the Pacific. In those fast-moving days which have intervened, the whole width of the world has passed behind us—except this broad ocean. I shall be glad when we have the hazards of its navigation behind us."

Amelia Earhart did not know of course that these were the last sentences she would ever write. She had, however, written a

Please know I am quite aware of the hazards. I want to do it - because I want to do it. Women must try to do things as men have tried. When they fail, their failure must be but a challenge to others.